GW01397888

Black Bird

by Aurora Dawn

DORRANCE
PUBLISHING CO
EST. 1920
PITTSBURGH, PENNSYLVANIA 15238

Dorrance Publishing Co
585 Alpha Drive
Suite 103
Pittsburgh, PA 15238
Visit our website at *www.dorrancebookstore.com*

ISBN: 978-1-6853-7045-9
eISBN: 978-1-6853-7894-3

This is not a story, but a cycle.
A collection.
A jar of memories, set in amber
And fossilized in words.
It's about a journey,
Not just mine,
About what it means to heal
Grow
And change.
It is an evolution.

'Blackbird singing in the dead of night
Take these broken wings and learn to fly'

2013

May 23:

A fleeting thought crossed her mind for only a split second as she thought solemnly of the future, and it was enough to knock her flat on her back.

'You won't have to worry about that,' whispered the demons from the back of her mind, 'because you won't live to see it.'

And then the floodgates opened, sobbing hard and quiet, heavy tears grasping at the makeup that clung to her eyelashes and pulling it with them.

As she cried she wondered, who was she crying for?

The dead?

Or herself?

And what was the difference

Between them?

December 23:

God is in the people you push away.

2014

January 6:

I do this thing where I snap my fingers. I don't realize I do it, I don't know why I do it, I just have to. Maybe I'm trying to bring you back, like with a snap of my fingers you will magically appear. What would you say if you did? What would you do?

I keep having the same dream, where I run into you where we first met. Sometimes, you grab me by the neck again and I don't fight like before. I know if I touch you you'll go away again, but sometimes the urge to feel you again overwhelms me and I reach for you and you pull away from my fingertips. Sometimes I see you sitting there, where we first talked, and I can tell you're sick of me. I see it in your eyes. You hate me because I won't play along. I hate me too, because I do this to keep you here. I won't fight back because I need you to stay.

'You have to let me go,' you say, sitting with your legs apart and your forearms on your knees. 'This isn't healthy.'

'I don't care,' I lie. 'Why won't you let me touch you?'

You sigh at me. I can't look at your face anymore. I'm losing the small details, but I feel your stare of disappointment.

'You forgot what I feel like. This isn't real Aurora.'

I love and hate the way you say my name. I keep my eyes fixed on the people that aren't there anymore as you stare at me. Out the corner of my eye I see you stroking your thumb the way you used to mine and it makes me feel like someone hallowed out my heart with a melon baller. I wonder if you dream about me as I watch our memories play out all at once, different us's at different times like scars.

Suddenly I'm at your house. I'm at the counter and the house looks asleep. The light looks like a grey morning and I know you're waiting for me in the living room, cigarette hanging from your hungry lips. I know if I walk to you I'll either be hurt or kissed, so I walk in the only direction I know, and when I see your face from the end of the hall, my fingers snap and I'm awake.

January 6:

It's the coldest it's been in 20 years on the way to my father's. I want to cry, but my tears would freeze and crying never did any good, did it?

It's the coldest it's been in 20 years and everyone feels the need to remind me as if I can't feel the bitter slap of wind when I open the door.

I can't fucking stand small talk.

It's the coldest it's been in 20 years and gathering my things has become the hardest imaginable task lately. My bones creak and muscles freeze as if resisting on their own. All I want is to curl up in my bed, listening to my mother laugh from the living room. Her laugh has always been obnoxious, but beautifully contagious, the same laugh as mine.

She rarely laughs anymore.

Instead I'm sloppily folding clothes and tossing them into a bag, while my mom makes gentle conversation with the man that hurt her on the phone as he makes his usual demands. The children, money, insurance. It breaks my heart in a way I can't properly describe. I wonder if she ever wants to say 'I love you' before hanging up the phone. I wonder if she ever did.

It's the coldest it's been in 20 years and the goddamn car won't start. I set my bags in the tiny kitchen and close my eyes, imagining all that I'm leaving behind. Mom picks up her keys and lets out a sad, sigh-like 'I love you' and I whisper it back, not able to bring myself to look at those tired, empty eyes of hers. If I do, I know we'll both start to cry. It's the coldest it's been in 20 years and I think it's an omen I should take heed of, but I stay quiet and wait for railroads. There's only two this way. She slows before the first one, she knows how upset I get when I miss one. Little remnants of the one that hurt me. Strange the way some habits form. I put my fingers on the icy window as we roll over and quickly slip my hand back into my pocket as we resume our solemn drive. I'm ready for the second one, my stupid little ritual to hold on to you, and as we go over I think of hell freezing over and laugh because, look around, it has, we're driving there ourselves.

It's the coldest it's been in 20 years and as we park silently in my father's driveway. We trade 'I love you's again, and I joke lightheartedly because I can feel us both sinking. As I step out and crack the sheet of ice that has become the driveway and fight a lot more than just the cold to make it to the door. I don't look back because I'll cry, and then my tears will freeze. besides, crying never did us any good anyway.

January 9:

I decided long ago
That I didn't deserve to breathe
So I'm holding my breath
Until you come back to me

January 16:

There is no sleep for the girl in the clouds
She's up all night to make sure
She
isn't
falling.

April 1:

Baby skin, old eyes, and a cigarette addicted to her
What a joke.

October 22:

My hands are either too hot
Or too cold
My head is on fire
My heart is freezing
But my love
and this goddamn coffee
are room temperature.

November 26:

I'm trying so bad to not tear at my skin.
Shove my nails into my flesh.
You packed your bags
And placed them under my eyes.
I'm not surprised
Everyone leaves.

December 5:

My chest is so heavy
One part chest cold
One part heavy heart.

December 18:

When people leave you cling to things that can't leave. Old sweaters and blankets that once held warmth and a scent, but now are cold and smell like nothing. Songs you danced to, or sang to each other, that now leave you sick to your stomach. Pets that don't understand why you're sad or why there's less occupants in the house. Forgotten and abandoned items that fill you with so many emotions, too many to describe, because

In a metaphorical sense

You're the same.

December 26:

I talked to your mom. I wonder if she knows. The way she looks at me, the way she lingers when we hug, tells me maybe she does. She knows you better than you think, we all do. You're predictable as always. I was just selectively blind. I didn't want to be right. It's your fault.

Why me?

I never deserved the nightmares. The haunting of those oh-so-cruel-but-gorgeous eyes. Your voice gives me chills still. Your soft fingers and your nicotine tongue invading me even now.

I still miss you.

It makes me sick.

You don't deserve me.

I never deserved you.

I still love you.

I'll always hate you.

2015

January 17:

I'm so sick of crying with no one there to tell me that everything's going to be okay.

A lump in my throat and a stone for a heart

Your frown is all broken in

You're making this so hard.

January 26:

I never really wanted any of the cigarettes or glasses of wine
 I was just looking for peace in a place
 I knew how to find
 Like mother, like daughter.

January 28:

There is a black spot growing
In the center of my heart
With her name in
bold

January 31:

I'm not stable
Sane is off the table
But I can love you
Like a daydream
In the middle of July

February 20:

I'm still not afraid to die
But I'm no longer afraid to live.

February 27:

I'm falling in love with the way the sunlight casts pale shadows
on my bed
    And how the birds talk outside my window
    About coming home too soon

March 15:

I heard birds this morning
Singing songs of coming spring
The sweetest music in my ears,
Still ringing,
But just as real.

March 16:

I thought it was love
because you made me feel like I was standing at the edge of
a skyscraper.
You made me feel like I was flying
I only just realized
I'm afraid of heights.

March 26:

I told you I love the stars
But little did you know
I love the ones that made you the most.

March 30:

It's all grey until the sun settles down for the day
And the shadows drag out their last sigh before night
Melting oranges and dusty blues take over the sky
And yes,
I do love this place
Wait till sundown
And I'll show you why

March 31:

The sun is right outside my window,
and he walks right in as if he knows the ground
He takes a look around and says in a sigh,
'Quit breaking hearts
It won't fix yours'

April 7:

1:39 A.M.
Give me something good
I'll find a way to fuck it up

May 18:

I want to be the brightest I can be
So that when you close your eyes
I'm all you see.

June 23:

I awoke to the loudest thunderstorm an hour ago
Now I'm listening to the rain
And giving up on a rainbow

July 2:

You were cold and salty like the ocean, bringing me in and spitting me out. I breathed you in and you pulled me down. Now my chest is on fire and my head is exploding because you're living in my lungs like smoke and water.

July 3:

2:31 A.M.
How will I fuck this up.
How do I not fuck this up.
I can't fuck this up.
What do you see in me?
Why would you pick me?
Fuck,
I'm glad you did.

July 4:

I am a firework exploding in midair,
leaving nothing behind but smoke
and a ringing in your ears.

July 5:

Our anniversary
My skin is humming everywhere your touch lingered
And I'm going mad at the thought of being away from you.
This is a whole new feeling.

July 6:

I fell asleep with tears in my eyes
And woke up
With my head in the clouds.

July 7:

(1 am)
I wrote the words I was too afraid to say on your skin
And hoped you didn't notice
But also prayed you did.
Either way
I hope you don't leave.

July 8:

You picked up my heart
And dusted it off
Like an old book:
You sat down
And studied every page.

July 12:

Maybe if I just lay still and close enough,
We will just become one
And never leave each other again.
My roots grabbing on to yours
In the slowest and most beautiful dance in the universe
Until we are so entangled in our vines
That we can't tell whose heart is whose,
But it would never matter.

July 17:

This isn't real
This isn't happening

July 18:

The way you touch my skin,
Like a canvas waiting to be painted;
How you kiss my stomach,
Like it holds new galaxies:
And the way you look at me,
Like seeing home after a long trip.

2016

May 6:

There's a different kind of light pouring in today. I'm not sure where it came from, but I hope it stays.

October 22:

If you can't love and accept the most important people in my life
Then why are you in mine?
You don't get to pick and choose which parts of my life you want to acknowledge
and ignore the rest.
Find your Goddamn priorities.

2017

January 17:

All of my emotions are so specific and yet
So vague
Like I can't quite articulate them the way I want to
And always end up disappointed with the result
Which is why I don't write anymore
Except for this, I guess,
But I have feelings that are much more than feelings
They're more like moments,
Like scenes in a play;
Except it would be a terrible play
Because no one else would understand it
Like the way I feel when I look at my husband
Is a gruelingly long
'Look at you, you're incredible'
That makes me want to cut open my insides and smear
them onto the walls
to write 'I LOVE YOU' with every single piece of me.
I want to break each one of my bones and make a mosaic
out of them.
I want to give him my ribcage and my collarbones and my
pelvis and paint them his
favourite color and say,
'Here, they're yours'
But that's impossible
And gross
And weird
And I don't know why I feel that way but emotions don't
make sense.

When I look at my best friend
I feel this weird feeling of belonging mixed with love and
tainted with sadness
I feel the way old books smell
Really well-loved books, your favourite book.
And when I think about her I think of those sunbeams
that pierce the clouds in the winter
and make me feel warm and cold at the same time
Like hot cocoa in a log cabin
Like a fire with friends in the middle of the night
Like laying on the bathroom floor after a panic attack
I want to string together stars and pour them on her head
I want to make the perfect painting and draw her inside
the life she's always deserved
I want to take out my brain and put hers in my skull
Give her my body so she can see herself the way I do
I want to give her all the love I have for her
So that she'll finally love herself.
When I think of my ex
I feel a lot.
At first I feel sick.
Not like, 'I'm going to vomit' sick
More like, my organs shut down sick
Like this is the sickest you can be without dying sick
Right there, teetering on the verge of life-and-death sick.
Like I can feel his hands on my neck again sick.
Then I feel angry.
I feel like ripping out my esophagus
I feel like my blood could turn to venom.
Or burn so hot that it burns through my skin and pours
out slow and thick

Like lava
I feel like my jaw could turn to stone
And like my skin needs a new layer
So I should rip off at least two.
I never want to think of him again
But he haunts my brain like the way the smell of cigarette
smoke
Clings to your clothes
I want to live without a throat
So my head could just float there
Disconnected from me
Hanging midair like a balloon
Because feeling is tiring
Because even when I can't feel I feel like I need to feel harder
I feel like none of this makes any sense
But I felt it.

January 25:

I used to think that being tough was about
Bloodied hands and scuffed elbows.
Broken noses and bloodshot eyes.
I know now that my strength is in gentle hands
And soft embraces.
Kind words and tearing eyes.

January 26

I'm writing again.
I write why I'm crying.
It's a lot less than before.
I'm eating again
And finding new ways to make myself full
I get sick much less often now.
I'm writing again.
Writing for you.
It's all for you.

January 27:

'Until death do us part'
Is stupid.
I will be with you long after I'm gone.
Long after the earth reclaims me.
Long after the sun engulfs the earth.
I will love you until the universe collapses and explodes
And I will love you more
When it's all rebuilt again.

February 11

It hurts so bad to see your face turned away
Or your eyes closed,
I long only for those deep greens to get lost in mine
Like they did when they first discovered them.
I ask only for your attention
Undivided
In moments uninspired.
Hear me crying in the night, escaping your bed
And hold me.
I hate crying alone
But I always run and hide.

March 30:

I'm so afraid
I'll never balance the chemicals in my brain
And they'll be the reason
You'll walk away.

May 18:

I am so tired of disorder
I'm tired of not being good enough
Not to your standards, but my own.
I'm tired
I'm tired.
I'm so tired.

June 6:

I can't live like background noise
I cannot live like background noise.
Please, I'm begging you
Turn to me, talk to me, connect to me
I miss our summer
And I fear
You'll never love me like that again.

June 27:

I am a storm
The sky
And the sea
You are only a ship.
I won't let you have control over me.

July 23:

Let me be the rain that makes you shiver to your core
Let me be the motherly warmth that holds you until
you're whole again.

August 10:

I'm not sure what I thought I'd find here;
A circle
A thought
A hope
Or a fear.
I know it's uncertain,
But the future is near.

August 15:

My father taught me
To speak softly
And carry a big stick,
So my words are like dripping honey
And my knife
Is always sharp.

September 20:

I will never stop trying to find new ways to tell you
That I love you

September 26:

Let go of your grief
This life is so spectacular
So random and short
I don't want to miss a single second.

November 30:

If you looked hard enough before you'd find suicide notes
Now there's vows
Hidden in notebooks
Scattered love notes
Poetry scattered throughout my brain
Life tastes different in your embrace.

2018

February 24:

Can you honestly look me in the eyes and tell me
That you've never thought about ending it?
That it would be easier with someone else.
You tell me you still love me but you don't seem as happy
anymore.
You tell me you're not tired of me, but I hear the strain in
your voice,
Tired of answering the question,
And I don't believe you.

February 26:

Every now and then I hear the question
'If you could go back and tell yourself one piece of advice,
what would it be?'
I only have one answer.
Stay away from him.
You will know him the moment you lay eyes on him.
The one made of fire and brimstone, piss and vinegar.
He will destroy you.
You will rebuild, but god, will he rip you apart.
He will inject poison into your mind,
Hiss lies into your ears,
and cast a spell over you that will make those words
sound sweet.
For years, you will go away, be someone who is not really you.
He will empty out your chest and take up residence in the
cavity and when you refuse him
he will fill your lungs like saltwater.
He will drag you down and leave you lifeless in a cold,
vast, empty void where you'll
wait for him to save you for only a few moments at a time.
But if you don't, if it's already happened, if it has to happen,
By god, you have to fight.
Breathe in the saltwater, but exhale fire.
Bleed him from your veins.
Whatever it is that gives him control of you, be rid of it.
Rip off the flesh he touched and be raw, then grow back
tougher.
Scream until you cough up blood.

Be angry, be pissed,
Live out of contempt and spite.
<u>Fight</u>.
You will never be the same. Every year you will see that
date and your heart will sink.
You will hear that name and you will taste blood.
It's been 4 years.
And it's still the same,
But we're stronger now.
You will discover yourself again
Make a new you
And you'll breathe life into her all on your own.
YOU will string fairy lights through the cavity that remains
in your chest and invite
someone in and they will not enter until you tell them to
And you'll be whole again.
You'll find love,
Real love
And together you'll mend what has been broken.
Rebuild what has been lost.
It will always hurt
But you will be free.
You'll be safe.
You will find meaning and healing.
You'll learn that you are enough,
you always have been.

March 2:

I NEVER WANTED IT TO BE THIS WAY
I ONLY WANTED YOU TO LOVE ME
BUT THERE WAS A DARKNESS IN YOU THAT WAS
SPILLING OUT
AND MY CORNERS TURNED BLACK AND I KNEW I
HAD YOU LEAVE
BEFORE THE COLORS WENT AWAY AGAIN
PLEASE
UNDERSTAND I DID THIS FOR ME
I LOVE YOU
BUT I'M NOT SORRY.

2020

April 19:

Happiness is the color yellow pouring in over your thoughts
And trapping them in a nostalgia-flavored amber.
It's an ease of life in waves of laughter and color,
A letting go
A release of tension and grief even if only for a moment.
It feels like a friend remembering something vague about you
Or like a kiss on the forehead when your lover thought
you were asleep.
It feels like a warm late-summer evening
And a breeze from an eventual storm rolling in
But not now, not yet.
Right now there's still children laughing throughout the
neighborhood
And barbeques and bonfires smoldering
And gentle stillness in the air.
There's a momentary peace
And it must be inhaled in its entirety.

May 16:

Words have always been my ally
It is my tongue who betrays me.

June 5:

A porcelain doll on a shelf
A caged songbird
A flower, picked and dying
A piece of fruit, picked too soon
Father, mother, self-doubt, ex-lover.
All these things
I am not.

June 6:

Here I am
From my very core.
Take it.
It bears more fruit in your hands
Than it will ever will in me.

June 7:

What if
I grow only to accommodate.
I only exist to support.

June 8:

Simplicity is not in my nature.
I collect and I keep.
I find meaning in all things
And hold them tightly to my chest.
Things cannot leave.
Things cannot betray.

June 8:

For Zephyr
You're a different kind of sunshine
A different kind of love all together
I thought my life had changed a thousand times before
But they were ripples compared to the ocean of you.
How can someone so small take up so much space in my heart?
I can't tell if you changed my life
Or if every moment was building to the crescendo of you.
Thank you for existing.
I'm sorry I'm not more.
Thank you for making me want to be.

June 9:

I've never allowed myself the frivolity of hope.
It always seemed to me
like a story children tell themselves to sleep at night
Something to fill the void.
I had no room for hope.
Nothing solid to live for.
I couldn't bear to allow it.
Things like that
Go away.
Hope can be a weapon,
Taken away.
I steeled myself, hardened my jaw,
Sharpened my tongue against the stone of my heart.
But I am softer now,
Tearing down walls,
Planting flowers where once there was rubble.
Maybe it's time
To chance it.

June 13:

It's hard for me to hold back my nature
Wanting to reach out and hold the hand of anyone telling
me their troubles.
Wanting to feed every mouth walking in my door because
Who knows when their next meal will be?
I tell myself
Kindness is my life blood
It pours from my soul.
But I leave none
For me.

June 15:

Guilt

Sometimes I'm so wrapped up in my own world
I miss the most obvious.
I was told to write about guilt;
Your face appears.
Guilt is a feeling I keep hidden deep beneath virtue
Keeping my kindness on display to hide the flaws beneath.
I am not allowed flaws.
But there is a rot growing deep within me,
In the darkest caverns of my self-hatred,
When I didn't see the signs.
I was too self-involved
I let your pain inconvenience me
As if I was the one
Starving away to oblivion.
I'll never forgive myself for putting myself before you.
Maybe it's why I break myself bending for others
Giving everything I have left and more
Reading into every nuance to be sure they are safe.
I am sorry.
I'm so sorry.
I'm so sorry that memory hangs like an anchor from your chest
I'm sorry that I let it happen again, and again
You're my blind spot.
The memories hang like an albatross around my neck
I'll carry it forever to remind myself
You are more important
Even when you think you're not.

June 17:

Some people grow apart,
I had you surgically removed.

June 18:

The weight of the world on my shoulders
And yet,
I bend
To pick up yours.

June 19:

Isn't it so much easier for you
When they're docile?
Showing their belly at the slightest change in tone?
I've grown
The weight on my back hardening me
My skin calloused
I do not buckle.
Never again
Will I trade my silence
For your conscience.
I fear more than the loss of you now.
I'm sorry if that makes me cruel
No, I'm not.
I will not be meek
I see the way you look at the change in me.
You do not like it
But I do not care.
I do not exist
to please.

June 19, part 2:

I said no
You heard please
I screamed no
You stopped listening.
I made myself into the word no.
Carved it into my bones
Formed new skin from steel
Stood tall.
I am not weak anymore.
Whatever you ask of me,
The answer is no.

June 20:

It rains when I cry.
You don't notice.
I shake and swallow the sobs
Regain control
The thunder rumbles deep
'The weather affects our emotions'
You try to reason with logic
But the sky shatters when I scream.
It's so much harder to ignore the power
When it's making the house shake
But you knew I was a force of nature.
You said so when you met me.
If you didn't want hurricanes
Then don't piss off goddesses

June 21:

I tore off my skin after I fell
Burned away the first layer
Scratched off the second
Shed the third.
From it, black wings sprouted,
Broken and mangled,
But patience is a virtue
And I waited
In my cocoon of leather and bone.
I fell apart and reformed.
'Take these broken wings and learn to fly'
Ah, if you only knew.
I was no caged bird,
No toy for you to play with.
I was angelic
Cursed
Fallen
Taken
Now I've made my curse my own.
I whisper the words aloud,
forcing my new form into reality.
In the inky black of that night,
I found power.

June 23:

What a wonderful surprise it is
To have lasted this long.
Waking up to two pairs of green eyes,
A matching set.
Feeling your hands on my hips
Not recoiling instinctively.
The biggest surprise
is me.
I'm not the same person I was
Not even a little.
I belong to no one.
and I hear a voice singing
And to my surprise,
It's me.

June 24:

Keep your eyes
Fixed on me
You watch me
As I spin
But do not notice
I am the sun.
You spin
Around
Me.

June 26:

I wonder if you still think of me?
Memories that don't belong to you
of my mouth and thighs
Hidden beneath the mattress.
If my name begins to spill from your mouth
As you bury yourself in another
Choose a partner with the same first syllable
So you can catch yourself before it spills.

June 27:

Use your nails to tear away the flesh
Push your fingers further in
Pull out your esophagus
And rid yourself
Of the lump in your throat
Forever.

July 5:

I'm so fucking empty
Can't you hear the echo?
I pour every drop I have
Into everyone else
I have nothing left
I have nothing.

July 8:

I do not want to be made
Of honey and glass
I want to be made from clay and moss
Magma and brimstone
I want to be made of earth.
I want to put myself together with my own two hands
And live in her forever,
So build yourself
With spiderwebs and scorpions
Put hurricanes in your eyes
Forge your bones from the iron in the earth
Build yourself to withstand this world
And still be the most beautiful parts of it.
Because honey has an expiration date
And glass will crack and crumble.

July 8, part 2:

You say that you aren't good enough
And I wonder,
what is?
Where is the line drawn in the sand
Or the sky
That says,
'Here,
Here is where you have to grow.
You must be this tall to be worthy
Of love.'

July 27:

'It's okay,' she says,
But the bump between her brows betray her.
Swallow hard to soften the rocks climbing up.
Emotions are a burden
Heavier than Atlassian shoulders
Shackled
Beaten
And bound.
I had to turn it off
From the source.

September 12:

I wear my heart between my teeth
So that none can break it
But me.
I never learned the art of subtlety
All or nothing,
All for nothing.

November 1:

Thunder rumbles in my chest
The crack reverberates
Through those around me.
Destruction and creation
Electricity in my fingertips
But no breath left
In my lungs.

2021

March 18:

I feel so silly
Writing words you'll never hear.
And I feel empty
Saying things you'll have to heal.
And I'm so sorry.
I wish I wasn't made this way.
But god, I'm trying.
I pray you'll give me the time of day
But this night feels like it will last forever
But I've never been good at waiting
And I've never been one for praying
I've never been good.
I've never
No, I've never
I'll never
I never have.

March 21:

I was never trying to fix you
Because I never saw you as broken
But I saw you drowning,
My other half,
I had to help you
Because water in your lungs
Is water in mine.
You used my body to climb ashore
Screamed at me from the other side
As water pulled me down
And I wondered
How you had any air left in yours
Unless I wasn't yours
At all.

March 24:

Saturn's return
You cannot build a home
On beams you're ripping out
Smashed in the windows
Broke down the door
So that you could come and go.
But I am chained to the floor.
You tell me to just up and go
My roots are tangled into you
Are you cutting me free?
Are you aware it would kill me?
Where do I start
And you end?
Yellow bird flying out the window
Leaving me all
Alone.

March 25:

The antidote to poison
Usually comes from the very thing that poisoned you
In the first place.
You take it, analyze it
Reapply that knowledge
To mend what was broken.
There's a lot of power in that.
Knowing that the thing that is killing you
Can be the thing that saves you.

There is another way.
A riskier way
Of sipping that poison
Slowly, constantly
Until you build a tolerance
But it will only kill you slower

That's where I've been for months.
Sipping the poison off your teeth
That you don't realize are sunk into my neck.
Slowly they retract
But the poison is in my blood.
The antidote lies in your tongue.
In the kindest words and exquisite ecstasy of your love.
Tell me there's still time to fix it.

April 5:

You built me an empire
Of sticks and mud
Flesh and blood.
You built up the walls
And in my gratitude
I didn't realize how you enclosed me.
No,
I did.
But I didn't mind.
I didn't need an escape.
I had everything I needed here.
I told myself,
'This is all that matters,
This is all for you.'
Time wore the foundation
And through the cracks
Whispers from vipers
I tried not to notice you
Clawing at the walls
But restlessness broke you.
How do you leave what you built yourself into
Without destroying it?
I believed this empire a gift
But I was blind.
A castle you cannot leave
Is a prison.

April 21:

I'm on new meds.
An attempt to balance the scales.
Another acronym added to the collection.
Wouldn't it be ironic
To choke to death on the handful of pills
I have to take each day
To keep me from choking on a bullet
Or an extension cord.
If the pills I take to order the chemicals
Got caught in my throat
Just inches
From its intended purpose.

April 28:

It's all better now
So why am I still sick to my stomach?
Unsure and insecure
Breaking apart slowly
Little private pieces at a time.
The way you break a bone in your hand
To escape handcuffs
The calm before the storm
I can't trust that it's not all a ruse
That it wasn't all an elaborate game.
I can't be naive enough
To let my guard down again.
Can't forget that I am not enough
Cannot relax
Hold this pose
I can't lose you
Not again.
Because next time,
It'll be me who cuts the cord
I'll pretend it was my choice.

May 24:

My hands shake
Not with fear,
But rage
When I hear your name.
I want to see you burn,
Fulfill your promises
And go to hell.
I will never let you win
This war is
mine.

June 6:

I've never been more afraid
Than when I thought I'd never hold your hand again
Never kiss you
Never scream for you
Only at you
Never thought I'd laugh again
I spoke only through tears
thought that would be the rest of my life
Never been more afraid than the rug was ripped
And I saw you still standing.

July 8:

What pasture is green enough
To make you hate our garden.
Love grows
Where it is watered.
I suppose then maybe,
It was a different shade of green.

July 21:

I think that I am healing.
Sometimes it's hard to tell.
But I'm told healing isn't linear.
I like my therapist
She laughs at my jokes and swears with me
(I'll book another session soon, I promise)
I'd be lying if I said I was good
After everything I've been through, how could I be?
But I think I'm okay.

July 23:

Persephone was not taken.
She was a goddess of spring
Have you ever seen spring?
Do not be fooled by her beauty,
She is more powerful than thunder.
She sows life from the death of winter with her fingers in
the dirt
She rips out the heart of the world and breathes life back
into it
She brings weather where there was wither.
Persephone was not taken,
She knew what she wanted.
She wandered.
She took.
Death lives in spring.
Creation, and destruction.
I want to be Persephone.
In love with her equal
In balance
Wild and uncontrolled
A downpour,
A fury of color and floral.
A force
Of nature.

July 30:

I listened carefully
To silence
For ages.
Solitude and I are old friends,
We knew each other well.
I slept alone for 7 nights.
I lived alone for 7 months.
So Solitude and I
We know each other well
I speak her language
she spoke mine
And so we conversed regularly
In silence,
Loneliness
My only companion.

August 7:

I entered adulthood
And began the game I'm meant to lose.
Every step forward—
A step back.
Money has always evaded me
Like magnets of the same polarity.
You can push them together hard enough
And they'll make contact
But can you maintain the pressure?

August 17:

Every day the load lightens
Bit by bit we leave it behind
But I wish you had my gift of words
And could speak an apology
In my language.
Actions do not speak
Louder than my fears.

August 21:

My mood changes
Like a fist through a mirror
With a crack I watch the reflection change
Spider webbed universes of me
I don't know any of them
Bits of glass in my hand
Knuckles broken
But I don't flinch
It'll heal
Patch it up
But the mirror is fucked.

September 3, 4 a.m.:

I think I love everyone
More than they love me
It wouldn't be a bad thing
If the difference wasn't deafening.

September 7:

I want to be who I needed when I was younger
But the world does not want that person to survive.

September 16:

It's dangerous to wonder what it would be like
If I wasn't me
I wonder if she's happy
If pain eats at her from every corner at all times
If she can walk
Outside
And do more than just survive.
Being myself feels—
Sisyphean.
 as I hurtle back towards the earth I wonder
Why the hell I'll climb back up again
When will this cycle
Finally kill me?
Let the Boulder roll me over.
I think I'd find the pain of death
To be dangerously close to relief.

September 29:

I wonder if you feel it
The anger that rips from me
In angry red lashes
In quiet bleeding pools
In a steady drip
I'm living in a tide pool
A shadow box of hurt
Banging on the glass
Nestled between a necklace and a ring
A blanket and a mug
A brush and a book
I stick my face underwater and watch the scenes replay
Over and over
Round and round
I'm bleeding in the water
It slips from my veins
Red and angry
Because I cannot heal
The wounds behind me.

September 30:

My spine sits
Encased in claws and embers
Anchors tied to each shoulder
Between each finger, knee, hip
Cement hardens
Slowly
I wake up and fight
I go to sleep
And I don't
I am twisted into knots
Best friends with a bottle of painkillers
I want to speak to you
But I'm underwater
One thousand pounds of pressure
Pushing me into myself.
It feels like
looking into the sun
I take the medicine
And it only closes my eyes
It's too bright to think
Too hot to breathe
There's no getting better.

October 18:

I was never truly mad at you
For the positions you put me in
I knew it wasn't your fault;
That a piece of you had been stolen
And you were just trying find it.
But it left me there.
With every new bend I found lava
growing in my belly
Rising up my throat
And when I came home to that empty home,
An earthquake shook me to my core.
Tectonic plates of anger collided inside-
And I erupted
The wet singed away my cheeks
My mouth spewed and bubbled
I became
Noxious
Poisonous
Because after I was done
Once the ground stopped shaking
And I could breathe
I realized I was
Empty.

October 25:

I understand now
How love can be oppressive
I tried to love you for the both of us
I tried to love you for the whole world
I gave every drop I had
I pulled magic from my veins and bones
To conjure more from thin air
Like water, I overflowed
And so I built a dam
I tried to baptize you
In a lake of my love
Held you beneath surface
Hoping you'd come out born again
I tried to wash you clean
Not because you were dirty
But because you were hurt
Like water, I erode
I tried to be more love than you could ever need
To erase the pain of love that came before
Or the love that didn't
I ripped myself to pieces
And made you put them back together
"That is love" I told myself
Hurting for someone else;
I was wrong.
I was wrong.

October 31:

You and I against the world.
Against all odds,
We came back stronger.
(Happy anniversary)

November 26:

The bruised come to me
Speaking of the injustices they faced
In the same house
I was raised
I try to kiss their wounds
With a jawless mouth
my bleeding heart in my hands
I had to sew together what was left of my flesh
From when I stood alone in the flames,
And you walked the other way.

November 27:

I had to stand in the fire of someone else's rage
I came out the other side determined to never make some-
one burn for my own failings.
I choose to be kind because I couldn't imagine making
someone I love burn because of me.

Since 2013 I have been compiling these entries. I've missed weeks, months, years of them. I've lost a lot of them, deleted even more. I mourn them every day, because this book is a mosaic of the best and worst things of my life. These writings have been my therapy, my escape, my way of bleeding too-big emotions into a palatable language to make other people understand; and if you do understand, then I'm sorry. I hope that you find solace in them. I hope that they make you feel less alone, and I hope that you can read them one day in the future and they won't hurt as badly, as they have done for me. I am not a professional writer. I have never even taken a creative writing class, but words mean a lot to me, and I had nothing else, so when my world caved in, I wrote.

When I was sexually assaulted, I wrote

When I wanted to kill myself, I wrote.

When I wanted to self-harm, I wrote.

When I thought my world was ending, I wrote.

When my life was exploding in joy, I wrote.

And this is it. At least, what I have left.

What I have so far.

I am ready to put this behind me, and what better way than to share it with someone who maybe, just maybe might need it. If you do, then know that I love you.

If you read through this book again, pay attention to the changes. The growth, the bleakness, the happiness, the healing and then the backwards stumbles. It's all healing.

That is healing.

You will heal too.

CPSIA information can be obtained
at www.ICGtesting.com
Printed in the USA
BVHW052305020323
659623BV00008B/63